For a baby who was supposed to die, but was healed by the Grace of God—this is a compelling and inspiring read. Olivia Eder takes us on the journey that began for her when she was diagnosed with CP. In spite of all the ups and downs of her condition, like a lighthouse beacon, her faith shines through, showing us that with God, nothing is impossible.

—AnneGale Nester
Author of the *Eye of the Hawk* series of Christian novels

# A Miracle of
# GOD'S GRACE

My Life with Cerebral Palsy and My Journey with God

*Olivia Ellen Eder*

A MIRACLE OF GOD'S GRACE
Copyright © 2020 by Olivia Ellen Eder

All rights reserved. Neither this publication nor any part of this publication may be reproduced or transmitted in any form or by any means, electronic or mechanical, including photocopying, recording or any information storage and retrieval system, without permission in writing from the author.

The content of this publication is based on actual events. Names may have been changed to protect individual privacy.

Unless otherwise indicated, scripture taken from the King James version, which is in the public domain. • Scripture marked ESV taken from The Holy Bible, English Standard Version® (ESV®), copyright © 2001 by Crossway, a publishing ministry of Good News Publishers. Used by permission. All rights reserved. • Scripture marked NIV taken from The Holy Bible, New International Version®, NIV® Copyright ©1973, 1978, 1984, 2011 by Biblica, Inc.® Used by permission. All rights reserved worldwide. • Scripture marked NKJV taken from the New King James Version®. Copyright © 1982 by Thomas Nelson. Used by permission. All rights reserved.

ISBN: 978-1-4866-1944-3
eBook ISBN: 978-1-4866-1945-0

Word Alive Press
119 De Baets Street Winnipeg, MB  R2J 3R9
www.wordalivepress.ca

Cataloguing in Publication information can be obtained from Library and Archives Canada.

*I would like to dedicate this book to God,
who has been my biggest support through this new adventure!
May He bless and use this book for His glory!*

# CONTENTS

| | |
|---|---:|
| Acknowledgements | ix |
| Chapter 1: My Beginnings | 1 |
| Chapter 2: My Mother—My Guide | 4 |
| Chapter 3: God Is Faithful | 6 |
| Chapter 4: My Elementary School Years | 7 |
| Chapter 5: How I Got to Know Christ the Lord | 9 |
| Chapter 6: My Commute to Spiritual Community | 11 |
| Chapter 7: Trusting God Even When It's Hard | 15 |
| Chapter 8: Be Honest | 17 |
| Chapter 9: College Years | 18 |
| Chapter 10: What Do I Do Now? | 22 |
| Chapter 11: My Dreams | 24 |
| Chapter 12: Following God's Plan | 26 |
| Chapter 13: Seeking and Surrendering to God's Will | 28 |
| Chapter 14: Part of God's Family | 30 |
| Chapter 15: The Fruit of the Spirit | 31 |
| Chapter 16: Who Am I? | 33 |

| | |
|---|---|
| Chapter 17: My Disability Doesn't Excuse Me from Serving Others | 35 |
| Chapter 18: Putting It into Action: Serving Others | 38 |
| Chapter 19: Questioning God | 40 |
| Chapter 20: Live Separate from the World | 42 |
| Chapter 21: One Way to God | 44 |
| Chapter 22: Joy Unspeakable | 46 |
| **Photos** | 47 |
| Chapter 23: Don't Worry About the Future | 51 |
| Chapter 24: My Way to Worship God | 53 |
| Chapter 25: Have a Willing Heart | 55 |
| Chapter 26: God's Protection | 56 |
| Chapter 27: God's Love Never Fails Me | 58 |
| Chapter 28: Having Assurance of My Salvation | 60 |
| Chapter 29: Loving God | 62 |
| Chapter 30: What I Fear Most Will Never Happen | 64 |
| Chapter 31: Walking by Faith | 67 |
| Chapter 32: Never Give Up | 68 |
| Chapter 33: God Blesses His Children | 69 |
| Chapter 34: My Travelling Experiences | 71 |
| Chapter 35: Family Reunions | 73 |
| Chapter 36: People Who Inspire Me | 75 |
| Chapter 37: Spending Time Alone with God | 77 |
| Chapter 38: Practicing Self-Control | 78 |
| Chapter 39: God Is My Strength | 79 |
| Chapter 40: Falling in Love with God | 80 |
| Chapter 41: From My Heart to Yours | 81 |
| Chapter 42: All People Are the Same | 82 |
| Chapter 43: Educating Others about Disabilities | 84 |
| Chapter 44: Encouraging Others to Walk with God | 85 |

# Acknowledgements

**I want to especially thank my parents and my friends** Natalie and Rob for their encouragement and help in completing my book! A special thank you as well to my brother Alex who has been promoting my book and to all other family and friends who have supported and prayed for me in any way through this process!

# Chapter 1

## My Beginnings

**It was early in the morning on August 25, 1994 when my** mom and dad were faced with one of the biggest challenges of their life. They had to face the reality that their first child—a little girl—might not live through the night! My parents were told that I had experienced oxygen deprivation and was on life support.

Being a new mother, my mom was so worried that she called her church to pray that her baby would make it through the night. The members of our church prayed, and God heard their prayers. I was healed and ready to go home a few weeks later. The doctors and nurses at the hospital that had seen me nearly die were very surprised, except for one nurse who knew that God was bigger. I am alive today because of Him.

As if this experience wasn't enough for my parents, a number of months later, my mom noticed that I wasn't developing motor skills like other babies, so she took me to see the doctor. God gave them another test to try their faith—that's when they learned that I had something called cerebral palsy. This meant I was only affected physically and not cognitively. I would be confined to a wheelchair and would need help with all the activities of daily living.

My parents own a business, and as I grew my mom was very busy with looking after me and working at the same time. By the age of two, it was clear she needed help. So she prayed and God answered, but not how she expected. One day, she got an unexpected phone call from a lady who went to our church. When I got older, that lady, Natalie, told me her side of how she came to work with me.

After five years of working for a company, Natalie's job was eliminated. She was devastated because she and her husband had just bought their first home and she didn't know how they were going to afford it. She had lost her job early in the spring after accepting a promotion at work. She had prayed about the decision and now she was angry, confused, and questioning God. With tears she prayed that God would give her another job, but she didn't expect the answer she received either. In a few days, she got an overwhelming urge to call my mom and offer to help with me.

She didn't call right away because she had no experience with kids with special needs, but God reassured her that she could do it! She still hesitated—she doubted herself and was scared. She talked it over with her husband to see what he thought of her working with me and about her doubts as well. To her surprise, he encouraged her to call and obey God. So that evening she got up the courage to pick up the phone and call.

My mom was stunned when she picked up the phone and heard that Natalie felt led by God to help with me. My mother was unsure about Natalie, whom she didn't know very well. However, after she prayed about it, Mom decided to do a trial run. In the end, Natalie and I became good friends and have been together ever since. She is still one of my workers to this day—twenty-two years later! It must have been God!

Natalie and I had lots of fun doing many different programs. I was enrolled in Kindermusik, library programs, swimming, and Vacation Bible School. I had no desire to join programs that catered to special needs. So Natalie and I went to all the regular programs and we modified as needed. I miss those simple days.

Children are very open and accepting of those with special needs. I felt part of the group everywhere I went! Children are so innocent about people who look different. Oh sure, they may have lots of questions about disabilities, but once they understood more, they accepted me for who I was. I just felt like I could be myself with them.

## Chapter 2

### My Mother—My Guide

**My mother played a big role in shaping me into who I am** today! She looked at me as a child first, and only secondarily as a person with a disability. She didn't feel sorry for me, but always challenged me to do my best in everything. Of course, I didn't like it at the time, but you will see how she prepared me for school and how her prayers were and still are very appreciated and needed.

As a young child I went to physiotherapy every Friday in Toronto. It was a lot of hard work and sometimes painful to my muscles. My mom would push me to exercise every day, and my worker Natalie helped. Looking back, I am so thankful that my mom pushed me to do the physiotherapy. It's part of the reason why I sit up straight in my wheelchair. This isn't always the case for people with cerebral palsy. Many are more comfortable reclining as their muscles aren't strong enough to sit upright.

My mom encouraged me to do a regular program at school. This meant I had to work really hard to keep up with my studies, but ultimately it encouraged me to be more independent as I got older.

It was a new experience for me when she introduced different workers into my life. I had to get used to directing my care with people who didn't know me that well. This was definitely challenging for me because Natalie had worked with me since I was two, and knew all my routines, my likes and dislikes. The new workers turned my world upside down. I was forced to communicate all my preferences and routines. Fortunately, my mom was gracious enough to train them as best as she could—the rest was up to me! I was a little nervous at first but as I got to know them and got into my new routines, it has all worked out.

I have learned from my mom that people can't read my mind, so I am forced to communicate. Also, I'm learning to be more patient with people who don't know me; I can't expect them to know everything the first time they meet me.

Another thing that my mom taught me was not to be lazy. I know this sounds funny because I do have a disability, but I needed to learn to "earn my keep." After all, I was created to work, not to lie around! Sometimes I feel like I'm alone in this because a lot of people in my generation weren't taught to work hard and be independent. However, because my mom pushed me, I am now more independent and God has blessed me with two volunteer positions!

My mom has also taught me the importance of a prayer life. I know prayer is important to my mom because she prays for my brother and me all the time. I have applied prayer to my own life, and realize how important it is. Through her example, my mom has helped me grow in my relationship with God.

Even though our relationship has grown deeper and changed over the years, I will always love my mom for guiding me and helping me to mature.

## Chapter 3
## God Is Faithful

**Throughout my school years, people had doubts that I** could learn academically. You see, most children who have CP also have some learning disabilities. But not me! Of course, my mother had to fight in order for educators to give me a chance.

Can you believe it? With God's help, I even managed to win some awards. For example, I won the Carol Shantz Award, which is given to someone living with a permanent disability and attending post-secondary school. This was a miracle for sure! I wasn't even supposed get a high school diploma, but while there, I won the math, English, and parenting course awards. My previous church often quoted this passage: *"If God is for us, who can be against us?"* (Romans 8:31, ESV). This scripture is so true in my life!

# Chapter 4

## My Elementary School Years

**My mom had to advocate for me to go to a regular** elementary school. She spent a lot of time praying that everything would work out with my physical disability. It was a challenge for the school that I was to attend because I was the first to go there with such physical challenges, including my limited speech. But after many meetings and school visits, everything seemed to be in place for my learning.

Looking back, school was almost simple compared to the challenges that I face now. I've found it very challenging to find a job placement with my disability and speech limitations. That's not to say it wasn't tough at times in school—sometimes the workload was overwhelming, and before I got my power chair my educational assistant had to push me everywhere and I needed help with everything.

I made some friends in Grade Three and we became close through the years until Grade Eight. After that, the friends that I made in elementary school moved on and made new friends. Grade Eight was the last year I would see my friends, as the high school in my area wasn't accessible at the time that I graduated.

This was one of the hardest times in my life. I had to go to a different high school, and meet new educational assistants, teachers, and peers. No one knew me, and I had speech limitations. I think this is why I find it hard to get close to people—I never know when I might have to say goodbye.

As school became more challenging for me, I realized I needed someone to lean on. I'd gone with my parents to church every Sunday and sometimes through the week since I was a baby, but I knew I needed something real. I couldn't just go through the motions.

## Chapter 5

## How I Got to Know Christ the Lord

**As I got older, I started paying attention to the Sunday** school lessons and church services that I had attended since I was an infant. I learned about a man named Jesus Christ, who lived and died for the sins of the world. *How dumb is God?* I thought. *Why would anyone want to see their son Jesus dying?* Even though my parents had taken me and my brother (who is four years younger) to church every Sunday, I'd still missed the point. You see, I hate anything that is violent, so it turned me off. I didn't want anything to do with this crazy God!

It wasn't until I was ten years old that I finally understood the meaning behind the cross. One Sunday evening, I heard the same message—only this time I heard another voice. It was sweet like honeycomb, so rich that I knew it had to be God. "Don't be afraid of me," the voice said. "Please come to me."

"I have to go," I said to my mom. She had a quizzical look on her face, but I knew she understood. I had no time to explain, so I just went up to the altar and accepted Jesus as my Saviour. I understand that this may sound so cheesy and so simple, but God loves me just the way I am.

This was the beginning of my journey with God! Like any relationship, God and I have had some ups and downs, but He has never let go of my hand. He helped me get through my school years too. In high school, I had a support worker who was mean to me. All of a sudden, she started to yell at me. "You're not working hard enough and others are doing the work for you!" she screamed.

*Did I do something?* I thought. *Is she having a bad day?* I felt so alone and abandoned. The minute I got home, I cried on Natalie's shoulder. I felt frustrated with God, and I wanted to give up on Him because I thought He had given up on me.

Later, I found out that my school helper had reacted that way because she didn't like it when I talked about God with her. In the end, God gave me a new worker who was very nice and supportive. This experience helped me grow in my relationship with Him!

As if this wasn't enough, something frightening started to happen with my dad. I still don't understand what happened or if there is a medical term for it, but he was in a spiritual battle and needed help. He found a pastor that could help him, but the church was in a community by our cottage. We started attending every week, but it is about an hour and a half away from our home in Waterloo.

## Chapter 6

## My Commute to Spiritual Community

**FELLOWSHIP DISCONNECTED**
**I feel so disconnected from my spiritual community during** the week. I enjoy worshipping God with my friends at church on Sunday, but because of my commute, I sometimes feel more like an outside observer than a vital part of my spiritual community.

When I'm at home during the week, I'm not able to do anything with my church friends. This isn't building Christian friendships the way I'd envisioned.

As it is, my physical limitations with cerebral palsy complicate my ability to feel a vital part of any community. I have to communicate through a special device, and that takes a lot of effort for both me and for the person listening. This means it takes me more time than most to build meaningful relationships.

In my ideal world I would love to live my whole life in just one community. I imagine how much easier it would be to stay connected with people throughout the week and to actually meet up and spend time together. But this isn't the case with me for now. This is the tension I feel in my current commute to spiritual community.

## THE TWO WORLDS I LIVE IN

I live in Waterloo, but my family and I attend a church near our cottage. Even though it's an hour and half away, we try to be faithful to the church because my family and I feel that like God has called us to go there. At first, it was kind of a novelty going up there every weekend, but after a while it has became somewhat tiresome and disheartening.

Don't get me wrong, I love my church. Its members have taught me so well and supported me so selflessly. But it's so hard to keep connected and live life with my church friends there. My parents feel the exact same way that I do. Even though we have technology like Facebook and texting, it's just not the same as face to face.

The commute somehow seems to make time fly by faster. Things happen in my friend's lives without me being there. It feels like they're maturing without me; some are even married. Usually, we only have time to say a quick hi and bye at church, since they are busy with their own lives. But we take little moments to pray for and encourage one another.

I still try to remember Paul's words that teach me how to live in community with my friends: *"Finally, brothers, rejoice. Aim for restoration, comfort one another, agree with one another, live in peace; and the God of love and peace will be with you"* (2 Corinthians 13:11, ESV).

But I long for deeper connection. I feel this big disconnect from the church community when I go back home to my other world. I never know what is happening in the lives of my friends at church during the week, so I just pray for them as best I can.

**A TASTE OF COMMUNITY**

The reason I am longing for more connection is that at one time I did experience the benefits of living my life entirely in the same community. During my time at Bible school I was able to do things together with my friends throughout the week. I felt a little more a part of that community.

I was able to go with friends to special events such as retreats and banquets. It was so much fun being with my friends and just having time together for fellowship. Being with them during the week was like a joyful extension of the time of worshipping God on the weekend.

I suppose I should count my blessings. Natalie is a Christian, and sometimes I go to her church. I even went to her Bible study and met some young people. It's good, but I feel like I'm missing out on some opportunities, things like worship nights.

I know that as long as we travel, I will always struggle to find connection spiritually, but even in this struggle I can trust that God is at work. *"And we know that for those who love God all things work together for good, for those who are called according to his purpose"* (Romans 8:28, ESV).

I need to trust God. He knows my future and will guide my steps in His time. I hope that my story will encourage you to seek spiritual connection, no matter if it's limited ability or a commute that may hinder you. I know I don't want to miss out on deeper opportunities for spiritual connection and friendship.

Christian communities should also help you grow. To be truthful, my church is very strong in that. For example, before I went to Bible college, everybody prayed for me, like Ananias did in for Saul.

> *So Ananias departed and entered the house. And laying his hands on him he said, "Brother Saul, the Lord Jesus who appeared to you on the road by which you came has sent*

*me so that you may regain your sight and be filled with the Holy Spirit."* (Acts 9:17, ESV)

When they prayed, it encouraged me to know that my church was supporting me.

## Chapter 7

## Trusting God Even When It's Hard

**At my church, I have several friends, including a best** friend named Meghan. But it's so hard to stay connected with them since I live in Waterloo. Also, it feels like they are moving on with their lives without me. Some of my friends are married or dating, so I can't really relate to them on that level. When people ask me where I go to church, I feel embarrassed and ashamed because no one in their right mind would travel an hour and a half to some church! However, I try to be faithful to my church, even though I feel like an outsider looking in.

Of course, I'm not sure what God's plan is in all of this, but I'm taking one day at a time. I know that God is perfect and He will show me His plan in His time. Even though I sometimes feel so weary, I have to remember that God is in control and all I have to do is trust and obey Him! Sometimes it's hard to let go and let God have His way, but I know that His ways are higher than mine. This is why I love Him.

One thing that I struggled with as a Christian was the commandment that God requires us to be baptized by immersion. I have always been nervous to go under the water because holding my breath has always been a challenge for me. I ignored God tugging on my heart to follow this commandment after I was saved. I figured God would excuse me because of my disability. Boy, I was so wrong—He kept on reminding me of the verse found in Matthew: *"But Jesus beheld them, and said unto them, with men this is impossible; but with God all things are possible"* (Matthew 19:26). I finally gave in and obeyed His voice. A few years ago, my brother and I got baptized on the same day, and God did help me as He promised!

Now that I think about it, not only did I feel relieved that I obeyed God, but I felt guilty for not doing it sooner. The lesson I learned through this experience is that no matter how much you fear something, God always is there to help you face your fears and press on. I also learned that I have to be honest with God and open up to people about my feelings. This is really stepping out of my comfort zone because of my fear of getting hurt. But if I know God like I think I do, He always wants to test me. You see, I asked Him if I could have a boyfriend. I guess I should've been more specific in my prayer, because it didn't happen the way that I'd asked for!

# Chapter 8

## Be Honest

**One day I met a guy in a youth group for people with** disabilities. It was during my second year of Bible college. We met at a youth group called Youth 'n transition. He was very sweet, but I wasn't very attracted to him. However, he was bold and asked me out on a date. I agreed, because I wanted to experience dating. You see, I'd never had a boyfriend, and I'd basically given up on the possibility.

He was not a believer, but he knew about God. You have heard it said, "Honesty is the best policy." Well, it's true! I should've told him that I wanted to break it off earlier, but I didn't want to hurt him. However, God and my school worker had convinced me that it was the right thing to do.

This guy always encouraged me when I was in school, and we're still good friends, but I see the pain in his eyes every time I see him. I try to encourage him and point him to Christ!

## Chapter 9

### College Years

**My church is very strong about getting a firm foundation in** the Bible, so I decided to apply to a college in Cambridge. After a lot of prayer, I went to Heritage College and Seminary. I was so excited to get the acceptance letter. I ended up facing many challenges there, but despite all of that, I had lots of fun! God helped me get through those years, despite my limitations. My favourite course was Old Testament because of the professor. He was so excited about the subject that I felt exhausted by the end of each class.

Looking back, though, I would have changed some things. In particular, I didn't use my communication device as much as I should have. I still met some new friends, though I felt like I was looking through a window at them. We did the basics—said hi and bye—but we never talked about anything in depth. However, I took advantage of being with them whenever I could.

Navigating personal relationships in college was a challenging experience for me. Being confined to a power chair, I need a personal caregiver to help me with everything. To communicate, I use a device called a Dynavox. I especially use it for oral presentations and in social settings where people don't know me well.

When I got accepted into college, I didn't have a personal caregiver. I prayerfully posted the job on the internet, and was amazed when a Christian girl responded. She was very nice and loved me to bits! We became good friends. Yet it was the role of my personal caregiver that became a barrier for me in building friendships easily and effortlessly, like other students around me.

For the most part, I adjusted well to my new social environment at school. In particular, I loved going to the formal banquets that my school hosted. I was thankful I could experience some social connection with those around me. But given my speech impairment, most of my social interactions were somewhat awkward. I didn't realize it at the time, but I now regret that I let my barriers hold me back from talking more deeply with my friends.

The core of my regret: I wish I had communicated more directly with my friends. By default, I let my personal caregiver talk on my behalf. I could have used my speaking device, but to ease social tension, I deferred to my assistant. I allowed the awkwardness to prevent me from building deeper friendships with the people God had placed in my life. What depth of potential friendship did I forfeit?

Understandably, my caregiver was protective of me and was eager to speak on my behalf. Whenever friends approached me, I simply smiled and nodded and she would do the talking. Even though she was helpful in being my voice, at times I also resented her for taking over my conversations. In her desire to protect me, it often felt like she didn't want anyone to get to know me.

I now know that I didn't need to defer my social engagement to her, and that this is what made it difficult for me to bond with others. Sadly, it felt like everybody liked her more than me. After all, they were constantly talking with her.

However, my regret in my social interactions as a student doesn't define my future ability to build healthy relational connections with people around me. Here are some truths I learned on my journey.

## I AM A MIRACLE OF GOD'S GRACE

Looking back, it is a miracle that I even graduated from college given my physical disability. No one was confident I could do it, but God provided all that I needed! I am accustomed to overcoming challenges as I've always been the only one in my classes with a disability since kindergarten.

Since graduating, I have taken more risks socially and taken initiative to be more connected to others. I need to learn from the regrets of my college experience. I have a long way to go, but I trust God as I help others in their journey.

## GOD'S PROMISES GIVE ME HOPE

During hard days of relational struggle, I keep coming back to two verses.

Philippians 4:13 says, *"I can do all things through him who strengthens me"* (ESV). This verse always reminds me that no matter how hard it is to connect with others, God is always present and working His strength into my situation.

Matthew 19:26 says, *"But Jesus looked at them and said, 'With man this is impossible, but with God all things are possible'"* (ESV). This verse keeps me trusting that God can do what everyone thinks is impossible.

## I CAN SHARE MY STORY WITH OTHERS

I have turned my regrets into action. God has given me opportunities to share my experiences. Recently, I was able to share my story with children in a camp setting. There were some there who weren't familiar with what it means to have a relationship with Jesus. I hope that I inspired them to draw closer to God. Of course, they had a lot of questions about my disability, and I didn't mind helping them understand.

## I CAN MENTOR OTHERS

God has also given me opportunity to mentor two friends who also have disabilities. One has the same disability as me, and both friends struggle with depression. In my times together with them, I try to encourage them by sharing with them the hope that God has given me.

Finally, I want to encourage you, whether you have a disability or not, to keep initiating conversations that can build your personal relationships. Take social risks to become connected. Don't let anything hinder you from connecting with others. Consider what is keeping you from initiating socially with others, and how you can act on lessons learned from regrets of the past.

# Chapter 10

## What Do I Do Now?

**After two years of college, I finally graduated. I felt like** God was telling me to move on. Even though I was going to miss my friends, I had a feeling that it was time to go. The only problem was I had no idea what to do. After I prayed about it, I knew God was directing me to go to work.

"Okay, God—but where?" I prayed.

There is a place called KidsAbility where I went for therapy when I was a child. Once a week, I now volunteer in the resource centre there. I work on the computer, signing toys and books in and out like a librarian.

Before I started working there, I had to find another caregiver. My mother joined a group for parents with "kids" with disabilities, through which we hired a young woman. We get along very well and I love her so much. I even went to her wedding!

I also work for a non-profit organization called Power to Change at home. It's a funny story how I met them: one day, my college had a career fair, so I decided to go. My electric power chair wasn't working so well. It kept stopping and starting, and I was so annoyed by it! Suddenly, I saw the booth for Power to Change. The booth attendant thought I was interested in their organization because my chair stopped right in front of their table. Through this meeting, God opened the door for me to write articles for them. I never imagined that God wanted me to write for His kingdom. This really was a dream come true!

## Chapter 11

## My Dreams

**When I was a young girl, I always wanted to be a teacher.** Since day one, I have loved kids. I don't know why—maybe it's the fact that they just ask questions about my disability without hesitation. Sometimes I think that we, as adults, overthink things. Or maybe we are too careful because we don't want to offend someone. I don't mind answering questions about my disability. In fact, I prefer that over having someone stare!

My second dream was to be a singer because I love to sing and praise Him and I like to make people smile. Even though I'm not a perfect singer, I know that God doesn't care because it comes from the bottom of my heart.

I also wanted to be a writer. I liked creative writing in high school, but that was all I liked about English class. Who knew that God would pick my third wish?

There is one more wish that probably isn't in God's plan. I want to have a Christian boyfriend! I'm going to leave all of my dreams at

Jesus's feet and trust Him. Of course, I know that all of my dreams need to line up with His plan. I just have to follow and trust His method in this life journey with cerebral palsy!

## Chapter 12

### Following God's Plan

**Even though it seems like I have it all together, I'm still** human. I question God a lot! For example, on occasion I'll ask why I can't find someone who loves Him and will love me despite my disability. Sometimes God puts verses inside my head to remind me that He is in control—like Proverbs 3:5-6, which says, *"Trust in the Lord with all thine heart; and lean not unto thine own understanding. In all thy ways acknowledge him, and he shall direct thy paths."*

I'm growing and learning to trust God in every situation, and I'm trying to be content with what He has given me. However, I have struggled with the verse that says, *"Wait on the Lord: be of good courage, and he shall strengthen thine heart: wait, I say, on the Lord"* (Psalm 27:14).

I'm trying to be patient with God, but some days it feels like all I ever do is wait! Waiting on my parents or waiting for God to answer my prayers. Still, I have no choice but to go with the flow. As I continue my walk with God, I'm learning to let go and let Him have

His way. I feel like David in this Psalm—God is encouraging him to wait patiently on Him. God has to remind me to trust Him in *all* things.

You may be surprised to hear this, but I can be stubborn sometimes. But of course, God knows that. I can't believe that He is so awesome and loving that He has the patience to help me. My patience runs thin, but His is indescribable! *"Because thy lovingkindness is better than life, my lips shall praise thee"* (Psalm 63:3). If I want to really serve Him, then I have to seek His will in my life. After all, I believe this is why I'm here! God commands us, *"Go ye into all the world, and preach the gospel to every creature"* (Mark 16:15).

## Chapter 13

### Seeking and Surrendering to God's Will

**This is a topic that I'm very interested in: to know God's** will and then do it! Sometimes I've asked myself "Is writing really in God's plan for my life?" My flesh—and Satan—make me doubt what God had promised me, but God reminds me that the devil is a liar and that I should listen to Him only. 1 Peter 5:8b says that, *"...the devil, as a roaring lion, walketh about, seeking whom he may devour."*

I know that I have to resist the devil and keep my eyes open and on God. He will keep leading me, if I keep seeking Him first. Jesus said in Matthew 6:33, *"But seek ye first the kingdom of God, and his righteousness; and all these things shall be added unto you."* This verse always comes to mind when I'm thinking of doing something without asking God first. I can be stubborn sometimes, like a little child wanting his or her own way. But God is very gracious towards me. This is what the cross is about! I thank Him for His mercy and kindness to me. I hope to help others like God helps me.

One way that I can serve is to encourage all believers like Paul did in 1 Thessalonians 5:11: *"Wherefore comfort yourselves together, and edify one another, even as also ye do."* I have to obey this too, especially if I want to be a help to God's family.

## Chapter 14

### Part of God's Family

**It's so comforting to know that I'm a part of God's great big** family. My grandmother and I always talk about heaven and how beautiful it will be. She's in her nineties and she's definitely ready to go home!

As I meditate on how God loves me enough to let me to be a part of His huge family, I'm in awe of His mercy and love for me. I'm on my way home. I can't wait to sing along with the angels and to have a new body. But most importantly, I can't wait to see God and be with Him forever! In Revelations 4:8, John describes the throne: *"And the four beasts had each of them six wings about him; and they were full of eyes within: and they rest not day and night, saying, Holy, holy, holy, Lord God Almighty, which was, and is, and is to come."* I can't even imagine what that will be like! Until then, I will "bring forth fruit" and wait till God calls me home.

# Chapter 15

## The Fruit of the Spirit

*...the fruit of the Spirit is love, joy, peace, longsuffering, gentleness, goodness, faith, meekness, temperance: against such there is no law.* (Galatians 5:22–23)

**Sometimes I feel like God is testing me in this verse. For** instance, I have had to put up with a lot of problems with my technology over the years—and, let me tell you, it hasn't been easy. It's so hard to wait for the "professionals" to get their act together. Usually, I'm pretty patient with my joystick or with my computer when it's not working, but sometimes I just want to throw all of it into the garbage.

However, God knows my heart—He knows everything about me and all of my "buttons." I know that He made me just the way I am! But I also know that His timing is always perfect, and all I have to do is trust Him. This always is a challenge for me, because I want certain things done my way. It's my way or the highway. God has to keep reminding me that He is God and I'm not. Even though I'm in a wheelchair, I still have to surrender my will to Him, and I have to walk in the path that He has made for me.

# Chapter 16

## Who Am I?

**I thought it would be important to mention who I really am** and what I believe since the subtitle of this book is *My Life with Cerebral Palsy and My Journey with God*. My beliefs stand in between a Baptist and a Pentecostal (Bapti-Costal). You see, I believe in the manifestation and "empowering" of the Holy Spirit found in Pentecostalism, but I also believe in studying the Bible for yourself like a Baptist.

I believe that God never lets go of our hand, but I also believe that we can get distracted and walk away from Him. Still, God always draws us back to Himself. I know I'm probably not theologically correct, but this is where I stand. I'm not trying to offend anyone; I just want to be myself!

I am sharing this about myself because I want to be real and humble. I certainly don't have all the answers, but I know that I hate conflict in the body of Christ. Not only does conflict among believers cause hurt, but it hinders unbelievers from wanting true salvation.

I want to shine God's light with a right heart and be ready to serve others, even though this is challenging with my disability—or so I used to think!

## Chapter 17

### My Disability Doesn't Excuse Me from Serving Others

*As ye would that men should do to you, do ye also to them likewise.* (Luke 6:31)

**HOW IN THE WORLD?**
**Whenever I think about these words of Jesus, I ask myself,** "How in the world does he expect me to do this? Doesn't he see me? How can I possibly serve others when I myself am in a wheelchair? Am I not exempt from serving others because of my disabilities? Am I not the one that needs serving?"

His words have a way of rattling my cozy preoccupation with being served. They make me feel uncomfortable. They're so counterintuitive and countercultural. Perhaps that is why I still feel like such a novice at serving others. But against all odds, God is challenging and changing my attitude of complacency, helping me to do just that.

## ONLY BECAUSE HE FIRST LOVED ME

If I am ever going to take His words seriously, I first need to remember that He has always served me in the self-sacrificial way He calls me to live out. I am humbled to see how Jesus gave himself so selflessly for me. He had everything in heaven and could have lived eternally content serving Himself, paying no attention to me. Yet, He left all of his glory in heaven to give His life in service and sacrifice for me.

I never grow tired of contemplating the depths of His love for me. *"For God so loved the world that he gave his one and only Son, that whoever believes in him shall not perish but have eternal life"* (John 3:16, NIV). As a follower of Jesus, I am invited and empowered by Him to serve others with love, because He first loved me.

## A COSTLY LOVE

But God's love is far more costly than my notions of love. He calls me to help and serve people every day, not just when I feel like it or when I can receive something in return. To be honest, I am intimidated by the thought of following the selfless example of Jesus. He continually puts other people's needs first, ahead of His own.

How can I possibly deny myself and put others before me like Jesus did? It's very hard for me to do, especially since I live in a generation that tells me that my life is all about serving myself. If it was up to my efforts alone to achieve such selflessness, I would despair and give up. But I am seeing God's Holy Spirit at work, helping me put away my own selfish desires and put others' needs first!

When I use my disability as an excuse not to serve, it shows the motive of my heart is to put myself first. I can sometimes allow my inability to excuse me from my ability in the Holy Spirit. I have to adjust my expectations to be sure, but I can always do something to serve others.

**ALWAYS A WAY I CAN SERVE**

Despite my limitations, God is showing me there are always places I can serve others. I have been blessed to serve in formal contexts such as camps, Sunday school, and church.

But most of the time, I can find opportunities to serve in small and personal ways. Currently God has led me to encourage a younger friend in high school who has the same disability as I do. I try to pray for her often. I enter into her struggle with depression, and can easily remember what anxieties high school brought for me. I can relate to her, and help her navigate the ups and downs from a perspective of faith, hope, and prayer.

**NO ONE IS EXEMPT FROM SERVING OTHERS**

As you can see, God is showing me that my disability doesn't excuse me from serving others. I cannot give in to temptation and let my disabilities get in the way of obeying the words of Jesus and putting others before myself. Even though my service may be limited and I sometimes make mistakes, I am learning to imitate God's heart and serve people.

Finally, I have learned that serving others blesses me and gives me hope. When I help or encourage someone, it feels amazing! Sometimes they express that they are blessed, and I just feel like God is smiling down at me and cheering me on. I hope that you are encouraged to put others first, because I know what a blessing it will be for you to serve others.

Take a moment and think about how much Jesus sacrificed for you. What excuses do you use to convince yourself you cannot serve? In light of His example, His command, and His empowerment, consider how you can serve others, and—most importantly—think about them before yourself.

# Chapter 18

## Putting It into Action: Serving Others

**One example of how I serve others is to write them letters** of encouragement. God laid this on my heart about five years ago when a senior lady I knew was struggling physically, emotionally, and spiritually. I had known her since I was a baby, and she had always encouraged me through my life with a disability. She had been a Christian for many years, but about five years ago she became very sick and discouraged. I wanted to help her through this hard time, but I didn't know how, other than to keep praying for her. Since I can't drive or talk on the phone, I decided to do what I was good at—write!

After I spent some time in prayer, I knew it was the right thing to do. God showed me what to say and directed my hand as I typed. I obeyed His voice and sent a letter to her in faith, hoping it would encourage her.

After some time, she wrote me a letter back to thank me for the encouraging words, and included a verse from the Bible to encourage me as I had done for her. It became a habit for us to start writing to each other some words of encouragement and a Bible verse. At first her letters were short, but after a while they got longer and longer. This gave her something to do and kept her busy and made her feel needed.

It was amazing to watch God transform her and heal her gradually. There were many people praying, and her family was helping a lot too, but I also feel God used me to play a small part in her recovery.

One of the letters I got from her came with a special poem that stuck in my mind and has been a great encouragement to me:

> Yesterday, today, tomorrow
> Every worry, joy or sorrow
> God is in Control
> All the ones you care about
> Their wellbeing, and whereabouts
> God is in Control
> Your hopes and happiness and health
> Your welfare, work and earthy wealth
> God is in control
> All of life is Grace and Blessed,
> All that happens, for the best
> God is in Control.[1]

It's a good reminder that God is still on His throne and He reigns. I know that He has my future in His hands!

I still look forward to her letters and cards and words of encouragement. My prayer is that I can be used to encourage someone else who is struggling, and that God would shine through me!

---

[1] Author unknown

# Chapter 19

## Questioning God

**I have to admit that I don't have all of the answers in life.** From my past experiences, I think a lot of people assume that people with disabilities don't question things or have feelings because it's hard for those of us with communication barriers to express things verbally and articulate clearly how we view things.

I have lots of questions that God hasn't answered yet. For example, why hasn't God healed me? Or how come I don't see my loved ones coming to know Christ? But I will keep praying and seeking for the answers. After all, God said in Jeremiah 29:11, *"For I know the thoughts that I think toward you... thoughts of peace, and not of evil, to give you an expected end."*

These words are amazing to me because He is a good God who keeps His promises. All I have to do is put my trust in Him! Of course, it's easier to write that than to do it. But I know that God is always there to help me when I need Him. It gives me comfort to know that

He is there to catch me when I fall. It's also sobering to know that God is omnipresent and all-knowing, because I have learned that I can't hide anything from God and I have to be honest with Him.

## Chapter 20

### Live Separate from the World

**There are many people who call themselves "Christians"** but live the same as those who don't believe in God. I don't want anyone to be offended, so I'm choosing my words very carefully. In my opinion, I believe that there has to be a change in your heart. What I mean by that is, I can't say "I love God" but then go to a bar or something. Jesus said in Matthew 5:13–14,

> *Ye are the salt of the earth: but if the salt have lost his savour, wherewith shall it be salted? it is thenceforth good for nothing, but to be cast out, and to be trodden under foot of men. Ye are the light of the world. A city that is set on a hill cannot be hid.*

I believe Jesus is saying that I need to live like Him and shine my light before people. I understand that there are so many different definitions of a "Christian," so I'm going to use a different word. I'm a "believer" or a "follower of Christ." Paul explained it clearly in 2 Corinthians 5:17: *"Therefore if any man be in Christ, he is a new creature: old things are passed away; behold, all things are become new."* I'm not the same as I was before I met God because He's the One who made me new. He deserves all the praise and the glory!

Now that I really think about it, He turned my whole world upside down. I'm thankful, and this is why I love to praise Him. Of course, I know that God keeps changing me, and is helping me grow with Him.

# Chapter 21

## One Way to God

**Jesus said in John 14:6,** *"I am the way, the truth, and the life: no man cometh unto the Father, but by me."* I believe there is one way to God, and that is Jesus Christ. He is my greatest example of sacrificial love.

When I was little, Natalie took me to all different kinds of programs, including Vacation Bible School. I loved it, especially the music part! As I grew up, I even helped out in Natalie's class when she was a VBS teacher. I've learned a lot too. God has certainly blessed me. On top of that, He gave His Son for me. This is what I learned in VBS. Every time I'm with little kids, I'm reminded of Jesus' words in Luke 18:16–17: *"Suffer the little children to come unto me, and forbid them not: for of such is the kingdom of God. Verily I say unto you, Whosoever shall not receive the kingdom of God as a little child shall in no wise enter therein."* I want to trust God in that way, not caring about what people may think.

What God thinks is more important than pleasing people. In Exodus 20:5, God made it clear that *"Thou shalt not bow down thyself to them, nor serve them: for I the Lord thy God am a jealous God, visiting the iniquity of the fathers upon the children unto the third and fourth generation of them that hate me…"* This means that I should only worry about what God thinks of me and not about what people may think. I have to remind myself who I'm serving.

> *And if it seem evil unto you to serve the Lord, choose you this day whom ye will serve; whether the gods which your fathers served that were on the other side of the flood, or the gods of the Amorites, in whose land ye dwell: but as for me and my house, we will serve the Lord.* (Joshua 24:15)

I stand with Joshua on that!

## Chapter 22
### Joy Unspeakable

**I really believe that true joy comes from God. I'm not** saying that I don't ever feel down, because of course I do. However, even when I'm down, God gives me peace—a peace that *"passeth all understanding"* (Philippians 4:7). Even through the bad times, I can still have joy. It's only God that can fulfill me. For goodness' sake, I'm in a wheelchair, so what is there to be happy about? Well, I'm happy because of the assurance that I'm not walking through this life alone. I know that Jesus is all I need. It doesn't matter what life throws at me—I have an anchor that holds me.

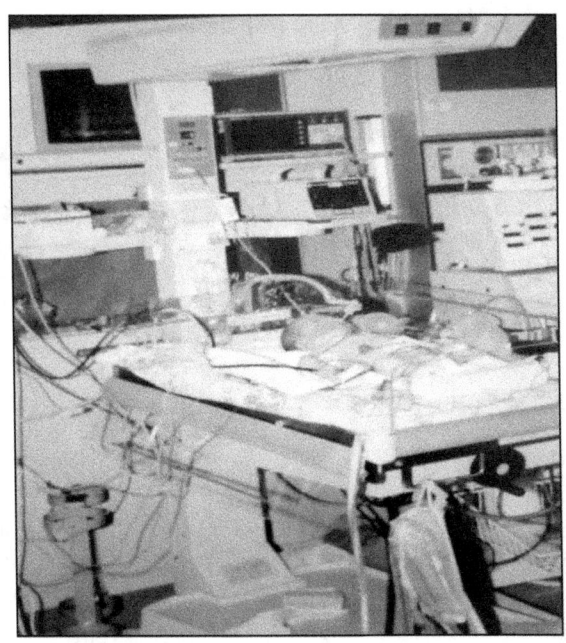

*I was transferred to London Hospital after nearly dying*

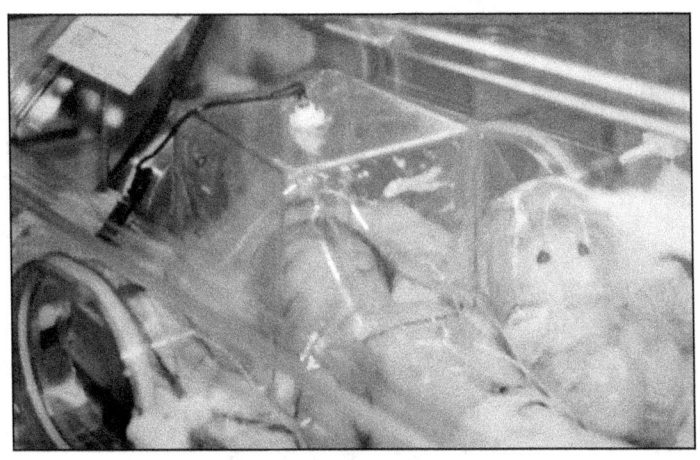

*My stay at London Hospital*

*My first trip to Disneyworld in my first wheelchair!
Also pictured: Alex (brother) and Natalie (worker/family friend)*

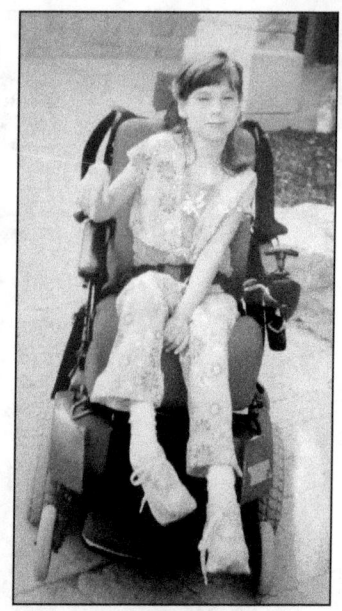

*My first power chair.
It was so exciting!*

*In my walker at the cottage*

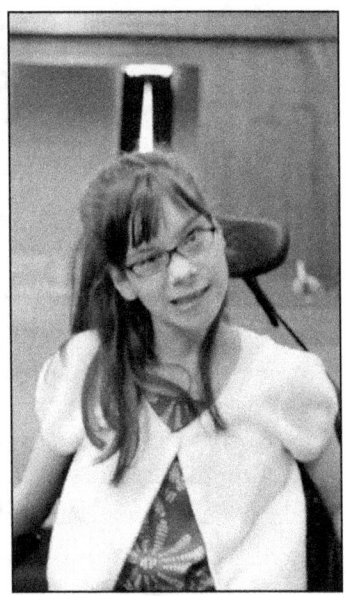

*Getting wet and having fun at New Life Camp as a volunteer!*

*Volunteering at VBS*

*My family. From left: Alex (brother), me, Della (mom), and Gary (dad)*

*High school graduation—a miracle!*

*Bible college graduation—another miracle!*

## Chapter 23

## Don't Worry About the Future

**Jesus said in Matthew 6:25–26,**

*Therefore I say unto you, Take no thought for your life, what ye shall eat, or what ye shall drink; nor yet for your body, what ye shall put on. Is not the life more than meat, and the body than raiment? Behold the fowls of the air: for they sow not, neither do they reap, nor gather into barns; yet your heavenly Father feedeth them. Are ye not much better than they?*

I think God is very clear on this. He has proven Himself to me over and over again! I don't know when I will ever learn, but being in a wheelchair and having limited speech gives me lots of time to think—perhaps too much time.

I hate the unknown. For example, I had a tooth that grew outwards instead of down, and the dentist said that I needed surgery. My mind was racing through the possibilities of what could go wrong. What if my dentist makes a mistake? What if something goes wrong with the surgery and I die? Of course, nobody dies from a tooth removal, but I was so scared that logic was thrown out of the window. In the end, God helped me and I didn't even have pain! I will try to trust God and not worry over things that may never happen.

Sometimes, I laugh at myself for being so clueless and crazy. Surely God has a good sense of humour to put up with me! This is why I have joy down in my heart. Nothing can take away the joy that He has given me. Despite the circumstance, I can still have *real* joy. Accepting Christ as my Saviour was the best decision that I have made, because He never leaves me, nor forsakes me. In Hebrews 13:5 the author says, *"Let your conversation be without covetousness; and be content with such things as ye have: for he hath said, I will never leave thee, nor forsake thee."*

Even though I still struggle with this, I've promised God that I will really try to trust Him! When I don't understand what He has planned, I want to still be able to praise Him, like King David did in the Psalms.

I remember a time when I wanted to be more involved in my church but didn't know what this was going to look like. Some days I didn't know why I was at my church, because I wasn't really serving the way I wanted to. I became frustrated, but God taught me that His timing is perfect and I had to trust and wait for the answer. In particular, I love music and wanted to use this love to serve Him, but I had to be patient!

# Chapter 24

## My Way to Worship God

**I've always loved music. I grew up with music in my home.** When my mother was a girl, she took piano lessons, so I guess music is in my blood too! Recently, I joined the worship team at my church. At first, the head of the worship ministry didn't know how it would work with my disability. Also, they didn't know what my motive was. Even though I was a little hurt at the time, I now see their point.

Of course, my mom came up with a plan. I've always been nervous about driving up to the front of the church, because I never know if my wheelchair will stop or not. When I was at my old church, I used to play the drums. I used to go up to the front and play the drums until the offering was taken, then I would go back to my "seat" for the rest of the service. It worked really well, so I'm doing the same thing now that I'm singing.

Another way I can worship God is through my writing. I want God to use my words for His purposes and praise! Just like all the people God used to write the Bible, my prayer is that God will touch lives and work through me. In Colossians 3:23 it says, *"And whatsoever ye do, do it heartily, as to the Lord, and not unto men..."* It's my desire to live for God and to be used by Him.

# Chapter 25

## Have a Willing Heart

**I want God to use me, but I have to be willing to be used.** I believe that He's not a God who forces people to serve Him, but He wants someone who loves Him. In Matthew 22:37, Jesus tells us, *"Thou shalt love the Lord thy God with all thy heart, and with all thy soul, and with all thy mind."* This is one of the commandments, and I believe that God looks at my heart. Now this doesn't mean that I don't fear Him, but that I respect and want to serve Him. It's a good kind of fear, like a parent and child relationship. In 1 John 4:19, John states that, *"We love him, because he first loved us."* If God hadn't loved me first, I know that I wouldn't have given Him a chance. I don't want to have a hard heart, so I'm asking God to keep my heart soft and sensitive to His Spirit.

I've also read in the Bible that God will command His angels to be with us in our times of trouble, and this is another way that God shows His love to us.

## Chapter 26

### God's Protection

**About five years ago, my worker and I were in a car** accident. It was in the summer before my second year of serving at a camp, and we were on our way to visit her mom. I was singing along with a CD and daydreaming when, all of a sudden, we hit the car that had stopped ahead of us.

I saw smoke coming up from the van. Perhaps it was just my imagination, but I thought I saw a wing inside the smoke.

I screamed, thinking I was dead. Suddenly, I felt a hand on my shoulder. It was just my worker. We are both alive today because God sent His angels for protection! When the tow truck driver came, he was shocked. He said that he had never seen anyone walk away from an accident like this. The van was totalled, and we had only bumps and bruises!

The Bible does promise that *"...he shall give his angels charge over thee, to keep thee in all thy ways"* (Psalm 91:11). We didn't know it at the time, but my brother and my friends at the camp were praying for us too! God is good all the time, and all the time, God is good. He must have a purpose for my life, since he could have called me home that day!

## Chapter 27

### God's Love Never Fails Me

**Sometimes, I forget how much God loves me. I look to** other people or things instead of Him—I guess I want something more than Him. But I have to keep my eyes on God, and not on people around me.

To tell you the truth, I'm afraid to get too close to anyone (especially people my age) because they always move on with their lives. So whenever I meet someone or hang out with my friends, I keep everything casual. Nobody knows this, but this is why I like to call myself a "businesswoman." Of course, God's challenging me to take risks socially, but I like to stay in my comfort zone. I still struggle with this, but I'm getting there.

Sometimes, I feel like I'm putting a wall up. I am always afraid people won't take the time and listen to my words, which are hard to understand. Even when I use my communication device, I feel awkward because it sounds robotic and people aren't used to listening to devices that communicate. This is why I have to rely on God more, and He will help me open up to people.

If I'm ever going to be an example of God's love, I have to follow the "Great Commission" described in Mark 16:15: *"And he said unto them, Go ye into all the world, and preach the gospel to every creature."* My desire is that I want to be able to witness for God freely and not have my speech limitations get in the way.

# Chapter 28

## Having Assurance of My Salvation

**One day, I was reading a devotion that stood out to me:** *"In whom ye also trusted, after that ye heard the word of truth, the gospel of your salvation: in whom also after that ye believed, ye were sealed with that holy Spirit of promise…"* (Ephesians 1:13). I have to have a "know so" salvation—and I don't just mean head knowledge, but knowing for sure in my heart. This is all part of walking with God. I strongly believe that this helps with temptation and whatever Satan throws my way. Even though I may lose out on what people may call "fun," I know that I will get a reward in heaven. My hope is built on my Rock!

Just like the wise man who built his house on the rock, I have learned that I have to build my life on God. That means I need to imitate God's character in my life. I know I have to lean on Him, especially with my physical challenges.

Another lesson in God's Word that I learned is that if I put others before myself, then I will be a better witness for Him! Sometimes,

God reminds me that life isn't all about me and that I should check my attitude. I don't want to be the hypocrite that Jesus describes in Matthew 23; I just want people to see how much I love Him!

# Chapter 29

## Loving God

**Even though I have so many obstacles and challenges, I** still love God. Not only is He my Heavenly Father, He's my best friend. He is also my Redeemer and my Maker! This is why I try to love others and want to please Him. I will also continue to follow after God. Just like the Psalmist says, *"Let all those that seek thee rejoice and be glad in thee: let such as love thy salvation say continually, The Lord be magnified"* (Psalm 40:16).

Jesus emphasized these words in Matthew 22:37: *"Thou shalt love the Lord thy God with all thy heart, and with all thy soul, and with all thy mind."* I will continue to love Him because He never stops loving me!

My prayer is for people to see Jesus Christ in me. Sometimes it seems like they only see my wheelchair and don't see me as a person. However, I know that God sees me as me, not my disability. This is why I want to tell people what God has done for me.

I also know that I'm a sinner and don't deserve His grace. As Paul said in Ephesians 2:8, *"For by grace are ye saved through faith; and that not of yourselves: it is the gift of God: Not of works, lest any man should boast."* It's God's will that all would come to know Him, and it's a free gift.

As you can see, I'm not giving up when life gets hard, but embracing it with God. I hope that people will see that I love my Heavenly Father and that they will encourage others not to give up, but love one another. I'm practicing what Jesus said in Luke 6:37: *"Judge not, and you will not be judged; condemn not, and you will not be condemned; forgive, and you will be forgiven"* (ESV). I want to have that attitude towards people!

Another part of God's love is helping us face fears in our lives. I have had to face several fears in my life, and I am so glad I have had God helping me work through them!

# Chapter 30

## What I Fear Most Will Never Happen

**MISTREATED AND ABANDONED**
**In a moment, my worst fears materialized. I had to face** them all at once. What did I fear more than anything? I feared being mistreated, rejected, and abandoned by significant people in my life. My cerebral palsy only intensified my vulnerability and fears.

In high school, I was assigned a caregiver to help me. I assumed she would prioritize my well-being and always be there for me. That is why I was shocked when she started to act cruelly towards me. It was subtle at first but I could feel her increasing irritation with me.

All my worst fears became reality in a moment.

Looking back, I realized that I feared my caregiver more than God. I was prone to project my caregiver's actions onto God. I still struggle to trust God with my fears of rejection and abandonment, even after surviving this experience. Join me as I unpack my fears and trust God to help me walk through them in faith.

Fear: a distressing emotion aroused by impending danger, evil, pain, etc., whether the threat is real or imagined; the feeling or condition of being afraid.[2]

## WHAT I FEAR MOST WILL NEVER HAPPEN

Sometimes I fear that God will someday treat me like my caregiver did. In fear I question, "Will God lose his patience with me? Won't He also get irritated with me? What if He abandons me and writes me off, refusing to help me anymore?"

But as I grow in my faith (in God's Word), I am relieved to discover that God is patient and endures with me even when I experience mistreatment, rejection, and abandonment from people. It is a huge relief to know that what I fear most will never happen. God will never mistreat me, reject me, or abandon me!

## FACING REJECTION FROM PEOPLE

I have no doubt that I'm accepted by God, but not everyone responds to me the same way God does. Especially because of the physical limitations imposed by my cerebral palsy, I am still nervous to see how people will receive me.

Because I can only speak with the aid of a device, my speech is very slow. Even as I type on my communication device, I fear people will lose their patience and walk away. I struggle with the time it takes to explain myself. My inability to communicate effectively alone makes me want to curl up in a ball and hide from new people who don't understand me very well. I am tempted to give up before even trying. Every time I am about to meet new people, I need to rely on God to give me strength and boldness.

---

[2] "Fear," *Dictionary.com* (https://www.dictionary.com/browse/fear?s=t, accessed Oct. 8, 2019).

## MY FEAR IS GIVING WAY TO GOD'S LOVE

I remember the first time I heard the verse, *"There is no fear in love, but perfect love casts out fear. For fear has to do with punishment, and whoever fears has not been perfected in love"* (1 John 4:18, ESV).

This was once a foreign kind of love to me. It is hard for me to explain, but as I experience God's unconditional love, my fears are losing their power over me. Knowing God will never mistreat me, reject me, or abandon me gives me courage to face my lesser fears of being mistreated, rejected, or abandoned by people.

Now it's your turn:

1. What experiences have caused you to fear?
2. What fears are you giving in to?
3. How does it give you assurance that God will never mistreat, reject, or abandon you?

## Chapter 31

### Walking by Faith

**My faith in God is very important to me. Despite all of my** fears and uncertainties, I'm learning how to live by faith and not by sight. In 2 Corinthians 5:7, Paul wrote, *"...for we walk by faith, not by sight"* (ESV). Through my experiences, I've learned that I can't change people—only God can.

In the gospels, Jesus tells his listeners not to fear, but to trust. I know that I will get stressed if I'm not reminded of that, but God is always calm. Over and over again, He keeps reminding me that He is in control! Just like I had to trust Him with my salvation, I have to trust Him for everything else. I know that I'm far from perfect, but I will press on and continue to be Christ-like.

## Chapter 32

### Never Give Up

**As you have learned through reading my story, I'm** determined to live for God. Even though sometimes I'm scared of what lies ahead of me, I can trust Jesus. He knows everything that is going to happen, so I promise not to give up on Him! Actually, my favourite phrase is "never give up."

I know that God is my Rock and Shield. In Psalm 18:2, the Psalmist says, *"The Lord is my rock, and my fortress, and my deliverer; my God, my strength, in whom I will trust; my buckler, and the horn of my salvation, and my high tower."* I will continue to run the race as proclaimed in Hebrews 12:1: *"Wherefore seeing we also are compassed about with so great a cloud of witnesses, let us lay aside every weight, and the sin which doth so easily beset us, and let us run with patience the race that is set before us…"* I hope that others will be encouraged to run the race too.

## Chapter 33

## God Blesses His Children

**When I obey God and His Word, I will receive His blessings.** It's so simple that even a child can understand! Psalm 5:12 says, *"For thou, Lord, wilt bless the righteous; with favour wilt thou compass him as with a shield."* However, sometimes God has to discipline me before He can bless me.

Recently I had an argument with Him. I guess unconsciously I doubt His words and promises. Fear took control over me and made me want to take control. However, I've promised God that I will lay down all of my fears and questions at His feet and won't pick them up again! He is so real to me—now more than ever before. After the argument, I was reminded of Matthew 14:31: *"And immediately Jesus stretched forth his hand, and caught him, and said unto him, O thou of little faith, wherefore didst thou doubt?"* I felt so ashamed and afraid. It's a good kind of fear though. It's a respectful fear, because God is so good.

In 2 Timothy 1:7, Paul encourages us that *"...God hath not given us the spirit of fear; but of power, and of love, and of a sound mind."* It's a good reminder to practice what I "preach." I now realize that God knows my heart better than I do myself. In Jeremiah 17:9, the prophet writes, *"The heart is deceitful above all things, and desperately wicked: who can know it?"* I guess I can't count on my heart—only on God. I need to listen to Him instead of my own flesh, and put down all of my idols.

Even though spending time alone in God's Word is important, it is also important to connect with family and friends. I have been very fortunate to have had several vacations and adventures with my family.

## Chapter 34

### My Travelling Experiences

**When my dad was young, he used to travel a lot. I have his** personality, so I like to travel too. Even though it's a challenge with my CP, I still like it. For example, almost every year at Christmas, we take a trip to Florida. For a couple of trips, my brother, my dad, and I actually flew down. I loved it because it's so much faster than driving and I can keep my daily routines.

Another time, my mom, my grandma, and I went to see the Ark Encounter. We had gone as a family to Creation Museum in Kentucky a year or two before they had built the ark, but this time it was just the girls. They made it *"...three hundred cubits, the breadth of it fifty cubits, and the height of it thirty cubits"* (Genesis 6:15). The construction was pretty accurate. I felt like I was in Noah's day! I recommend it to anyone who likes history. It's for the whole family, and I was impressed by the way they made it looked so lifelike. They even had real life animals!

The most important thing to me was spending time with my mom. Because I'm with my workers every single day, my mom and I don't usually hang out as often as I would like to.

## Chapter 35

### Family Reunions

**I love my family, even though I'm not close to them except** for my grandma (the one that I travel with). I'm blessed to have both grandmothers alive, although I lost both of my grandfathers when I was little and I don't really remember them. But that's okay, because we will catch up in heaven!

Like I said before, I need to use my communication device more in social situations when visiting with my family for Easter, Christmas, and other get togethers. I'm just not motivated enough to talk to them! I have nothing in common with them. I know I should give them a chance, but it's just hard. Of course, I love them because I have to, but since none of my cousins have a disability, they don't know how to communicate with me. I'm a lot closer to my mom's side because she only has one brother (my dad has an older sister and an older brother, and I have lots of cousins on my dad's side, so you can imagine how noisy it gets). Some of my cousins try to get into my world, but again, I keep everything casual.

There are many people who aren't truly my family but have inspired me a lot. They have been very encouraging to me and have opened my world to try things I never thought I would have the opportunity to do.

## Chapter 36

## People Who Inspire Me

**My best friend at church is someone who inspires me.** She loves mission work, and was heavily involved in camp ministry when our family first came to the church. So, she encouraged me to volunteer at our church camp. She told me I could do it despite my disability! I never thought I would have an impact like I did. For example, when I was at camp, I met a little girl. For some reason, she was drawn to me like a little puppy following its owner around. She definitely wasn't afraid of me, and wanted to be with me all of the time! I loved her so much. We had lots of fun together. I loved the way she just trusted me without a thought.

My friend even asked me to share my testimony with the kids and teach a few lessons with my device. She was truly an inspiration in my life!

Another person who inspired me is a woman named Joni Eareckson, who is a motivational speaker and a writer. She's a quadriplegic, which means she is paralyzed from the neck down. I admire her faith in God and her perseverance. Even in her pain, she's still obedient to what God has called her to do. I hope to have that kind of determination to live for God!

## Chapter 37

### Spending Alone Time with God

**I encourage my readers to spend alone time with God. Don't** be like me, rushing through my devotions before my workers come. Even though it's rushed, I know it gives me strength and guidance to face the day. You see, all of my workers are talkers. No fault of theirs (I think it comes with the job description). Anyway, I believe this is important because it gives me strength.

I don't know about you, but I need God's strength every single day. Some of my workers tell me their life stories, so I have to sit there and listen. Not to boast or anything, but I think that this is the reason I'm such a good listener! I also think this is why I'm used to people talking *at* me, rather than *to* me.

Jesus said, *"Come unto me, all ye that labour and are heavy laden, and I will give you rest"* (Matthew 11:28). I know that without that rest, I would be defeated. But thanks to God, I can be recharged. I don't think I can help others if I don't go to the Source!

## Chapter 38

### Practicing Self-Control

**Do you remember in a previous chapter where I talked** about the fruit of the Spirit? Well, God has put that to the test! My brother Alex and a group of people from his Bible college went on a mission trip to Chile. Even though I had no desire to go there, I still felt jealous because Alex has this independent life that I can't even imagine! I had to swallow my jealously and be happy for him.

In Romans 13:13, Paul wrote, *"Let us walk honestly, as in the day; not in rioting and drunkenness, not in chambering and wantonness, not in strife and envying."* I know that I have to practice this daily—not just with my brother, but with my peers.

## Chapter 39

### God Is My Strength

**I feel God giving me strength every day, both physically** and spiritually! Living with CP can be draining, especially with all of my involuntary movement. Yet God is always right beside me. Just think about that for a moment. He has the power to help me to control my body!

> *What? know ye not that your body is the temple of the Holy Ghost which is in you, which ye have of God, and ye are not your own? For ye are bought with a price: therefore glorify God in your body, and in your spirit, which are God's.* (1 Corinthians 6:19–20)

I know that my body is the Lord's, and He'll strengthen me. Whenever I'm down, I will look to Him for strength. This is why I love Him so much.

# Chapter 40

## Falling in Love with God

**I know that I've already talked about loving God, but I** haven't talked about how much work it can be. All relationships take work, so why wouldn't it be different with God? I have to choose to love Him. In Mark 8:34, Jesus says, *"...Whosoever will come after me, let him deny himself, and take up his cross, and follow me."* So I need to "kill" my selfish desires and follow Him.

# Chapter 41

## From My Heart to Yours

**I have to be honest with my readers, so I'm going to share** one of my darkest secrets. Sometimes I wish I had a different life! What I mean is that I wish that I was able-bodied. I wish I could drive a car instead of waiting for my parents or the slow city bus! It would be weird to do everything for myself, but it would be cool if I could walk.

People sometimes judge me. For example, some people assume that I will never get married! Yes, it's true that this is an unrealistic goal, but I believe God can do anything. Even though I need to have helpers around me, I can live on my own and have a family of my own (if God wills). Also, it would be so cool if I didn't have to have help with the simplest things like my care. But still God made me for a reason, so I will zigzag through my life with Him.

## Chapter 42

### All People Are the Same

**Most of you have heard the saying "Treat others as you** want to be treated." What about those who are different? Does that apply to them? I have experienced not being treated the same as others because I look different. I would like to share with you how I handle being treated differently.

First, because I was born with cerebral palsy, I have lots of limitations. However, I'm only affected physically, which some people don't understand. My disability affects my speech and my movements, so some people assume that I'm mentally slow and they treat me like a child because of this. To be truthful, it's mostly the older generation—probably because of how they were brought up. I have to remember what Jesus said: *"You shall love your neighbour as yourself"* (Matthew 22:39, ESV). Even though I get so frustrated with them, I have to take a deep breath and ask God to give me more patience.

Secondly, I wish that others would see me as me and not just my wheelchair. What I mean is that I want people to ask me questions instead of staring at me. I'm really not at all that different. I have the same feelings as any other young woman has. I also know that I have to open up and use my communication device more. I'm determined to seek out opportunities to use my device and make meaningful relationships.

## Chapter 43

### Educating Others about Disabilities

**Sometimes I like to go back to my roots and share my story** to motivate others and teach them how to interact with persons with disabilities. I have shared my story with kids in Grades One, Two, Three, and Six. I hope to continue to share it with many different classes. I've said before that I love kids because they ask questions and want to learn without giving it a second thought.

I do my presentations with a communication device, which is a teaching tool to begin with. A lot of kids have never seen this before, and the voice is very robotic. People have to get used to this since more and more people with disabilities use this device. I even sneak in the fact that my faith in God is very important to me and has helped me achieve so many things in my life.

# Chapter 44

## Encouraging Others to Walk with God

**Finally, I would like to encourage my readers to have a** deep relationship with God. I can't imagine living my life without Him! He's my best Friend in the whole world. I can trust Him—He will be always there. No doubt about it, if I call upon Him, He will answer! Maybe not the way I expect, but He always answers prayers.

In Romans 12:12, Paul instructs the church to *"Rejoice in hope, be patient in tribulation, be constant in prayer"* (ESV). If God says that He can do anything, then I believe Him. After all, my favourite verse in the Bible is Philippians 4:13: *"I can do all things through Christ which strengtheneth me."* I know that I wouldn't even be here if He didn't have a hold on my life. There is an old hymn that explains it well.

> I'd rather have Jesus than men's applause;
> I'd rather be faithful to His dear cause;
> I'd rather have Jesus than worldwide fame;
> I'd rather be true to His holy name.

Than to be the king of a vast domain
Or be held in sin's dread sway;
I'd rather have Jesus than anything
This world affords today.[3]

This is my prayer: that people will give God a chance to make Himself Lord of their life. Jesus said in Matthew 11:28, *"Come unto me, all ye that labour and are heavy laden, and I will give you rest."* I'm not sure what the future holds for me, but I will trust Him until the end.

---

[3] Rhea F. Miller, "I'd Rather Have Jesus" (https://library.timelesstruths.org/music/Id_Rather_Have_Jesus/).

www.ingramcontent.com/pod-product-compliance
Lightning Source LLC
La Vergne TN
LVHW051527070426
835507LV00023B/3341